#4 in the Molly Learns Series

Molly Learns 10 Facts About Santa Claus

By
Marla Harms Judge
and Molly the History Dog

I0123231

I'm waiting for Santa to fill my stocking!
Do I hear him up on the roof??

For Bob – Thank you for all your love and support.

Book design by Jody Dyer and
Maria Loysa-Bel Nueve-de los Angeles

ISBN Paperback 978-1-958533-43-7
ISBN Hardcover 978-1-958533-42-0

Library of Congress Control Number: 2023915934

Please write to us at: Mollythehistorydog@gmail.com
Visit: mollythehistorydog.com

Crippled Beagle Publishing, Knoxville, TN, USA
crippledbeaglepublishing.com

"May you never be too grown up to search the skies on Christmas Eve."

Anonymous

Hi! My name is Molly.
I am a dalmatian dog.
I am white with black spots.
Most dalmatians have black spots.
But, did you know that some
dalmatians have brown spots?
One of my sisters has brown spots!

Holidays are such a fun time.
We get to see friends and family.
I love to go visit my friends,
especially my special friend, SANTA!

My family collects Santa figurines. I got to pose with a few of them.
Do you have a collection of special holiday decorations?

My human family and I enjoy traveling and visiting historical places. We like to learn about famous people in history.

The person we are going to learn about in this book is VERY famous, especially in the month of December.

This person has had many different looks and names throughout the years. Today we think of him as a plump man in a red suit with a white beard.

Did you already figure out we are going to talk about Santa Claus?

What a fun person to learn about!

The story of Santa Claus began a long, long time ago with a monk named St. Nicholas. People loved and admired St. Nicholas because he was so kind and generous. He helped people wherever he went.

Do you like to be a helper?
A helper is a special, wonderful friend!
I like to help whenever I can.
Sometimes I help pick up my toys.
What are ways you can help your family?

St. Nicholas traveled the countryside
to help people who were poor and sick.
Over the years he helped many children.
People described him as a kind man.
They began to have festivals each year to
honor him and all he had done.

When families left Europe and came to the
United States to start new lives, they brought
their traditions and holidays with them.

St. Nicholas was first introduced to the United States around 1773. A newspaper in New York reported that Dutch families who had traveled from Holland were holding festivals to honor his memory.

Through the years, St. Nicholas' name began
to change. To some he became just "St. Nick."
To others he was Kris Kringle. Here in the
United States, he evolved into Santa Claus.

Did you know that even today Santa has many
different names around the world?
I made a map of the world to show you
some of the different names he is called.

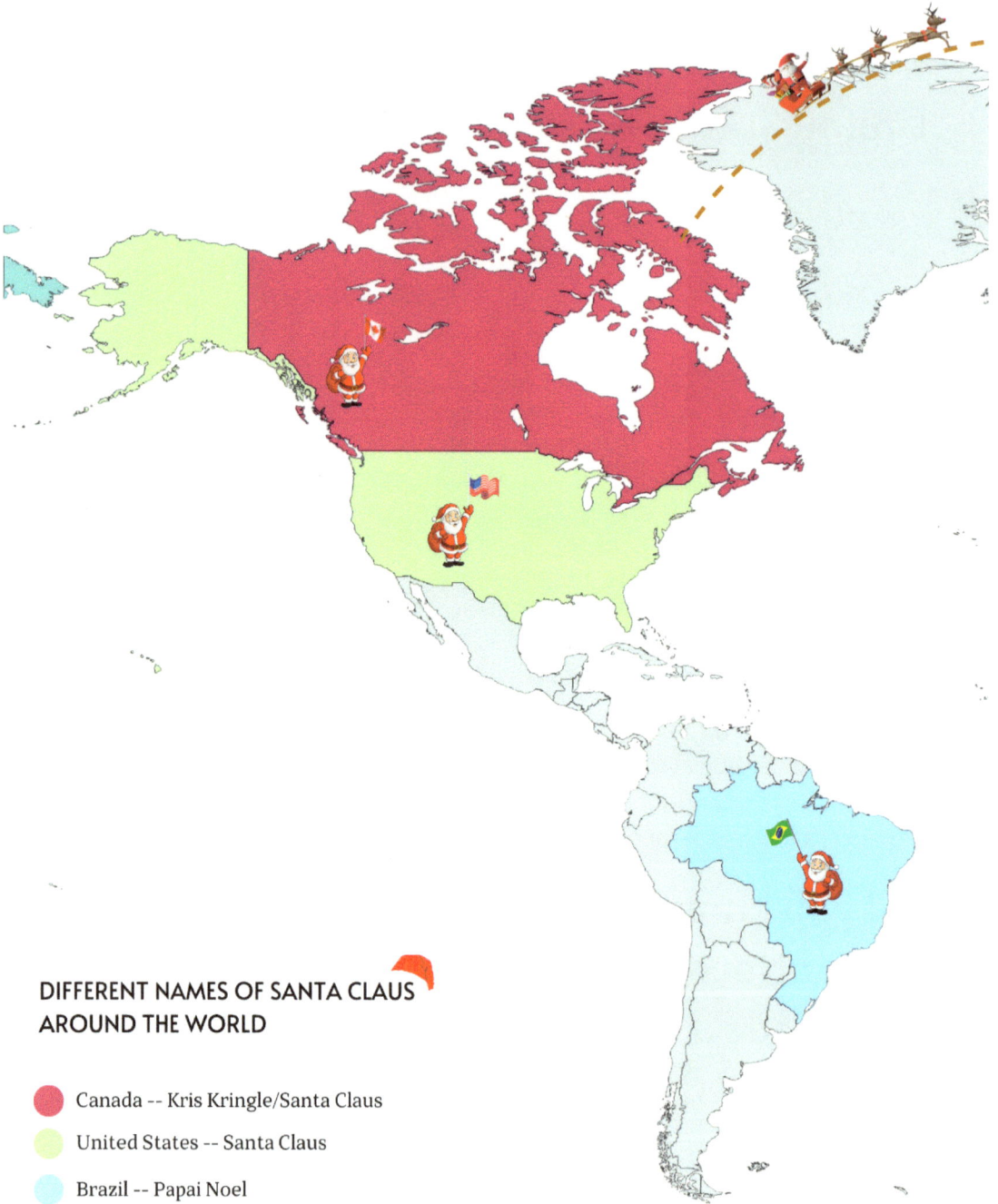

DIFFERENT NAMES OF SANTA CLAUS AROUND THE WORLD

● Canada -- Kris Kringle/Santa Claus

● United States -- Santa Claus

● Brazil -- Papai Noel

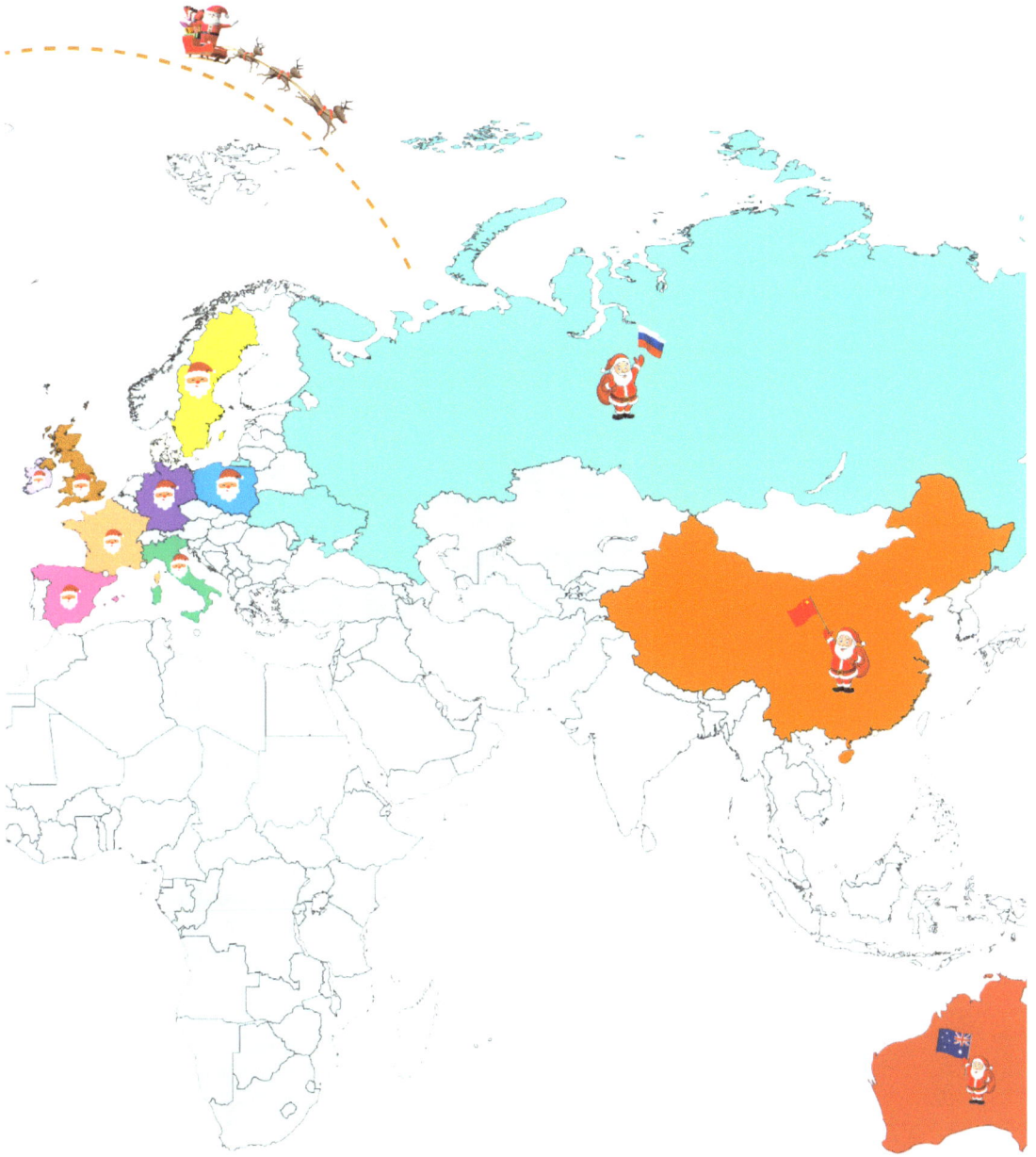

Sweden -- Jultomten

Russia -- Ded Moroz

China -- Sheng dan Lao ren

Australia -- Santa Claus

Italy -- Babbo Natale

England (UK) -- Father Christmas

Ireland -- Santa, Santee

Germany -- Weihnachtsmann

France -- Pere Noel

Poland -- Swiety Mikolaj

Denmark -- Julemanden

Spain -- Papa Noel

11

I learned about the different ways Santa looks, depending on where he is around the world. Would you like to learn about that, too?

For example, in the United States, he wears a red suit and hat.

In some other countries, he can look very different. I found some pictures of Santa in other countries. I thought you might like to see how differently he appears!

Netherland – Sinterklaas

France – Pere Noel

England - Father
Christmas

Russia - Ded Moroz and
Snow Maiden

Which Santa is your favorite?

Even here in the United States, Santa
has had many different looks.
When the United States was growing
and pioneers lived in cabins, Santa
looked a bit different than he does today.

A frontier Santa ready to make deliveries!

These boys portray frontier children enjoying Santa's visit!

During the Civil War, Santa wore a patriotic suit. I was able to visit with a living history interpreter portraying a Civil War Santa!

A fun visit with Civil War Santa

Soldiers liked having Santa look patriotic.
I think he looks wonderful!

This Santa visited children during what is called the Victorian Era.
The Victorian Era was named for Queen Victoria in England.
That was a long time ago in 1837-1901.

Santa in the 1920s

Children often visit Santa during the
Christmas season at stores and malls
to tell him what they would like
for him to bring them.
When I visited Santa, I gave him a kiss!

Children young and old visit Santa.
Most of the time they love sitting on his lap,
but some are a little frightened by him!
I have to admit, the first time I saw
Santa Claus when I was a young pup,
I was nervous!

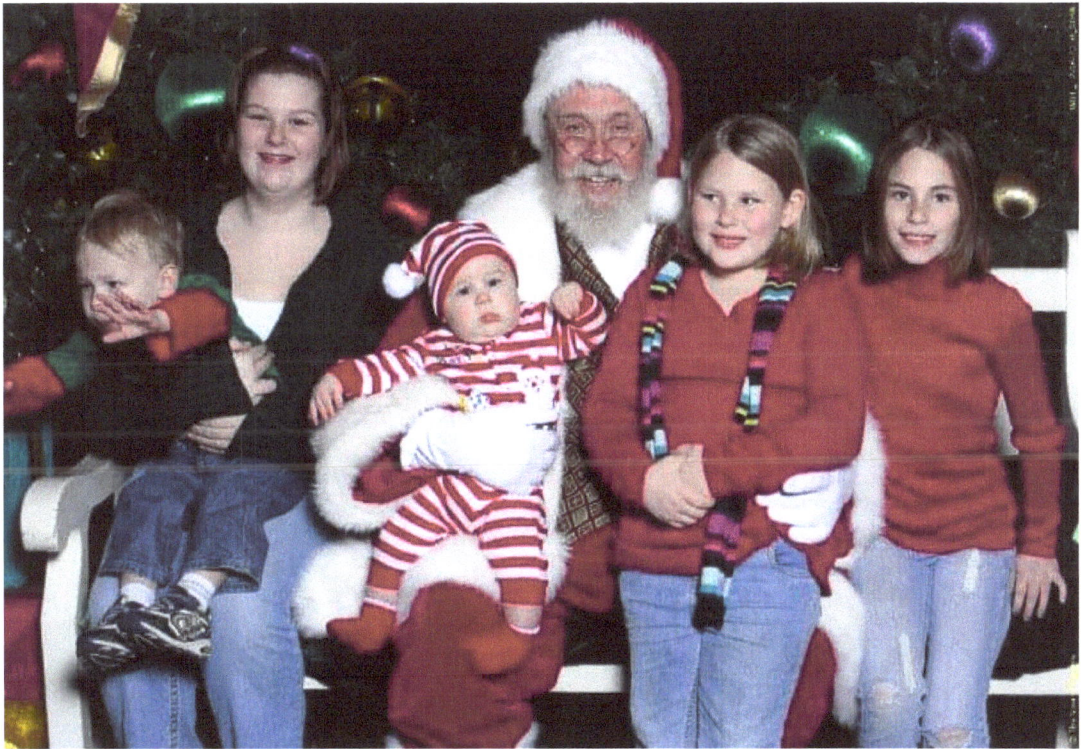

Children enjoy visiting Santa, well, most of them, anyway!

These children are much happier to see Santa!

Santa is such a famous guy.
Many stories, songs, and movies
have been written about him!

My family reads one of my favorite stories
every Christmas Eve. It is called:
Twas the Night Before Christmas.
It was written by Clement Clark Moore.
All the kids in our family gather around
Papa, and he reads the story to them.

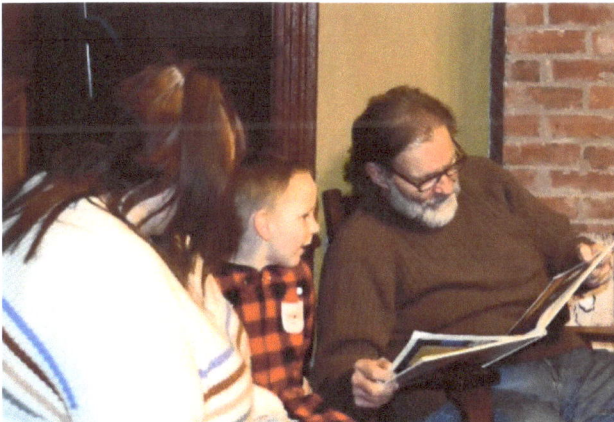

What do you like best about reading books? I like to look at the pictures that go with the story.

Picture from one of the many *Twas the Night Before Christmas* books!

Have you ever thought about writing your own story or poem about Christmas?
You could write about your favorite Christmas memory or your favorite gift!
I would love to read your story or poem.
You can have an adult help you send it to me on the computer by email.
My email address is:
mollythehistorydog@gmail.com.

At Christmas time, one of my favorite
songs to hear children sing is called,
"Jolly Old St. Nicholas."
Have you heard it before?
Here is a copy of the song.
Perhaps you would like to sing it.

Movies! Do you like to watch movies?
During the Christmas season, my family
and I watch many holiday movies.
Some of my favorite ones have
Santa Claus in them.
Do you have a favorite Christmas movie?
I think my favorite is called
The Christmas Chronicles.

Some children end up riding in Santa's sleigh!!
I think that would be AWESOME!

Another favorite movie of mine is called
The Santa Claus.
In this movie Santa falls off a roof and
a regular guy has to become the new Santa!
His son gets to visit the NORTH POLE!!

It is fun to make a bowl of popcorn
and sit with my family and watch
one of these movies.

A long time ago a movie was made
about Santa being kidnapped
by MARTIANS.
They took him to Mars to
help teach their children to
behave better!
I think it is a funny movie.

One of my favorite parts of Christmas
is baking all the yummy cookies!

I don't get to eat many because cookies
are not good for dogs, but I usually
enjoy a small taste.

Do you have a favorite cookie to bake?
My family bakes chocolate chip cookies,
snickerdoodles, and my favorite ones—
SUGAR COOKIES!
I like to make the sugar cookies because
we can cut them into fun shapes and
decorate them! Santa loves them too!

Want to bake some cookies?
I found a recipe for you to try.
Be sure to have permission to bake
before you start, and clean
up your mess when you finish.

Sugar Cookies

Ingredients:

1 cup softened butter

1 cup canola oil

1 cup sugar

1 cup powdered sugar

2 large eggs

1 teaspoon vanilla extract

4 ½ cups all-purpose flour

1 teaspoon baking soda

1 teaspoon cream of tartar

Gather all your ingredients,
wash your hands and get started!

Directions:

1. Preheat oven to 375 degrees.

2. In large bowl, beat the butter, oil, and sugars.

3. Add in eggs until well blended.

4. Stir in vanilla.

5. In a large bowl, combine the flour, baking soda, and cream of tartar. Gradually add to mixture.

6. Drop by small teaspoonsfuls onto ungreased baking sheet.

7. Bake 8 – 10 minutes until lightly brown.

8. Remove to wire rack to cool. Makes 5 dozen.

9. When cool, decorate!

Be sure to leave some out for Santa!!

Do you write a Christmas list each
year and send it to Santa?
Children send their letters to
Santa in many different ways.
Some children put them in
an envelope and mail them.
Some burn them up in the
fireplace and let the smoke
deliver the message to Santa.
I even watched a movie where
children sent Santa a video
telling him what they would like!

DEAR SANTA,

MY NAME IS _____

I LIVE IN _____

WITH _____

FOR THIS CHRISTMAS, I WANTED TO ASK YOU:

_____

_____

_____

LOVE,

However you decide to communicate with Santa you need to remember to be polite. Santa likes boys and girls that remember to say "please" and "thank you."

In our house, the children are allowed to ask Santa for one or two toys. Santa's elves have to make millions of toys each year, so we must not be greedy when we write our lists!

One other part of Santa's story we need
to talk about is his helpers, the elves.
Legend says they live at the North Pole
with Santa and make the toys Santa
gives to children around the world.
What a neat job that would be!

Like Santa, elves have had many looks.
Usually, pictures show them looking
like children with pointy ears!

Do you think you would like
to visit and help Santa's elves?
I think it would be fun to at
least visit Santa's home at
the North Pole!

Elves are pretty famous too.
There is even a movie about an elf!
It is called *ELF.*
Have you ever watched that movie?
It is about a human who grows up at the
North Pole and thinks he is an ELF!

I think it is wonderful that Buddy the Elf
becomes an AUTHOR!
He writes a story about his adventures.

Did you know that on Christmas Eve you can track Santa's trip using your computer?

If you log onto this website, you can figure out if you need to get to bed so Santa can visit you!

The United States government operates NORAD. Since 1955, children have followed Santa's flight using their technology.
I don't know about you, but I want to make sure I am in bed and asleep when Santa comes to visit my house!

Santa is on his way!!

Naturally, I wanted to learn all
about Santa's reindeer!
They are as famous as he is!
Do you know their names?
They are Dasher, Dancer,
Prancer, Vixen, Comet,
Cupid, Donner, and Blitzen!
Did you know that for a time
Donner was called Donder?
AND .. one more reindeer—
RUDOLPH!
Wow, Rudolph has his own
song and movies!

These reindeer live on a reindeer ranch in Illinois.

I learned some interesting facts
about reindeer. Would you like
to learn them too?

1 – Reindeer lose their antlers every year
and grow new ones.

2 - Reindeer make a clicking sound when they walk
and not just when up on a rooftop.
They have tendons that snap over bones in
their feet, and that's what makes the click.
Scientist think the clicking helps reindeer
find each other, especially in snowstorms.

3 - Mother reindeer usually give birth to a single calf,
although sometimes they may have twins.
Newborns stand up just one hour after being born
and can run faster than a human when one day old!

A newborn reindeer.

I have to admit, when I visited the reindeer ranch I was disappointed. I did not get to see them fly!

I guess that is something they only do for Santa on Christmas Eve!

Have you kept track of how many facts
we have talked about in our book?
These are the things we discussed:

1. The history of St. Nicholas
2. When Santa first came to the United States
3. Different names and costumes for Santa in other countries
4. Santa through history
5. Visiting Santa
6. Santa is in poems, songs and movies!
7. Writing letters to Santa
8. Santa's elves
9. Tracking Santa through NORAD
10. Santa's reindeer

What did you enjoy learning?
I think I liked learning about the
reindeer and the elves the best!

Christmas is such a fun time. I love
the decorations and all the yummy food!
I hope you have a wonderful Christmas season.

And look! While we were reading,
Santa filled my stocking!

Merry Christmas

A special THANK YOU to the Santas,
living history interpreters, and models
who allowed me to use their photos!
Lee Shafer
Robert Dickinson
Robert Judge
Hailey Judge
Katelyn Judge
Abby Judge
William Golladay
Samuel Golladay
Levi Beam

Other Books in the Series:

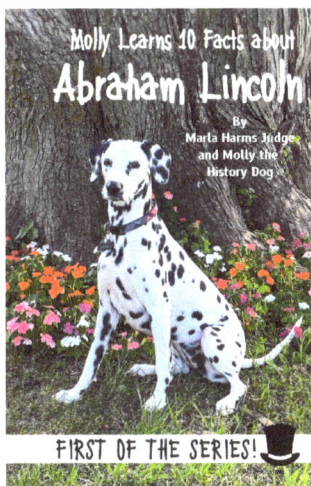

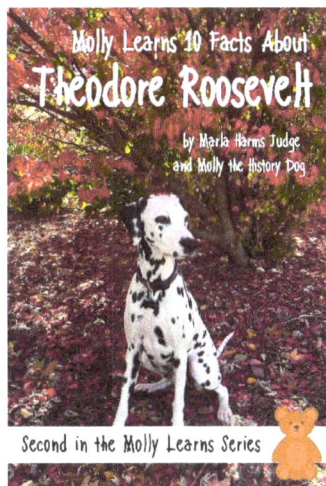

#1 Molly Learns 10 Facts About Abraham Lincoln

#2 Molly Learns 10 Facts About
Theodore Roosevelt

Finalist in the Theodore Roosevelt Association's Children's Book Award
2023

#3 Molly Learns 10 Facts About Mary Todd Lincoln

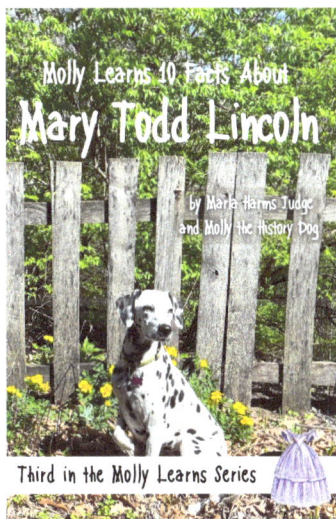

Visit us at: www.mollythehistorydog.com

About the Authors

Molly and Marla!

Molly is a beautiful, fun loving dalmatian.
She loves to travel and learn about history.
Marla is retired. During her working days,
she was a school librarian, a park ranger,
and a living history interpreter.
Her love of history and reading helped
create this book series.

A Fun Christmas Quiz!

1. The _____ are Santa's helpers.
2. The story of Santa started with St. _____.
3. Molly's favorite Christmas cookies are _____.
4. Santa's sleigh is pulled by _____.
5. What is Santa's name in France? _____
6. Children need to be in bed and _____ for Santa to visit.
7. What colors did Santa's suit have during the Civil War? _____
8. Santa's home is at the _____.
9. Christmas is celebrated on December _____.
10. What is Molly's favorite Christmas movie?

_____

REMEMBER! This is NOT a test!
It is just a fun way to see if you remember
some of the things in the story!

Answers:

1. The elves 2. Nicholas
3. Sugar cookie 4. Reindeer
5. Pere Noel 6. Asleep
7. Red, white, and blue 8. North Pole
9. 25th 10. The Christmas Chronicles

Great Job!

COLOR YOUR OWN SANTA

www.ingramcontent.com/pod-product-compliance
Lightning Source LLC
Chambersburg PA
CBHW060856270326
41934CB00003B/166